U.S. Regions

The Natural Environment of the West

Blaine Wiseman

MEDIA ENHANCED BOOKS
AV2 BY WEIGL™
ADDED VALUE • AUDIO VISUAL

www.av2books.com

AV² provides enriched content that supplements and complements this book. Weigl's AV² books strive to create inspired learning and engage young minds in a total learning experience.

Your AV² Media Enhanced books come alive with...

Audio
Listen to sections of the book read aloud.

Key Words
Study vocabulary, and complete a matching word activity.

Video
Watch informative video clips.

Quizzes
Test your knowledge.

Embedded Weblinks
Gain additional information for research.

Slide Show
View images and captions, and prepare a presentation.

Try This!
Complete activities and hands-on experiments.

... and much, much more!

Go to **www.av2books.com**, and enter this book's unique code.

BOOK CODE

E 7 3 5 5 4 2

AV² by Weigl brings you media enhanced books that support active learning.

Published by AV² by Weigl
350 5th Avenue, 59th Floor
New York, NY 10118

Websites: www.av2books.com   www.weigl.com

Library of Congress Control Number: 2014942112

ISBN 978-1-4896-1242-7 (hardcover)
ISBN 978-1-4896-1243-4 (softcover)
ISBN 978-1-4896-1244-1 (single-user eBook)
ISBN 978-1-4896-1245-8 (multi-user eBook)

Printed in the United States of America in North Mankato, Minnesota
1 2 3 4 5 6 7 8 9 18 17 16 15 14

062014
WEP090514

Senior Editor: Aaron Carr
Designer: Mandy Christiansen

Every reasonable effort has been made to trace ownership and to obtain permission to reprint copyright material. The publishers would be pleased to have any errors or omissions brought to their attention so that they may be corrected in subsequent printings.

Weigl acknowledges Getty Images as its primary image supplier for this title.

Contents

U.S. Regions

The five major regions of the United States are each a unique mix of **landforms**, climates, plants, and animals. The regions are divided by the natural landforms and environments that separate them. While they are different from each other, there are also many differences within each region.

Legend

- West (11 states)
- Southwest (5 states)
- Northeast (11 states)
- Southeast (11 states)
- Midwest (12 states)

The West borders the Pacific Ocean, Mexico, and Canada

The West covers 1,574,154 square miles (4,077,040 square kilometers).

Alaska

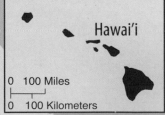

Hawai'i

CANADA

North
Dakota

Minnesota

Lake
Superior

New
Hampshire   Maine

Vermont

South
Dakota

Wisconsin

Lake
Huron

Lake Ontario

Massachusetts

New York

Rhode
Island
Connecticut

Lake
Michigan   Michigan

Nebraska

Iowa

Illinois

Lake Erie

Pennsylvania

New
Jersey

UNITED STATES

Indiana   Ohio

Delaware
Maryland

Kansas

Missouri

West
Virginia

Virginia

Kentucky

North Carolina

Oklahoma

Arkansas

Tennessee

South
Carolina

Texas

Mississippi

Alabama   Georgia

Atlantic
Ocean

Louisiana

N

Florida

Gulf of Mexico

0   250 Miles

0   250 Kilometers

What Makes the West?

The West is the largest region in the United States. It is known for its natural landscapes. Alaska stretches far into the ocean, where Attu Island is the most western point in North America. At Point Barrow, Alaska, marshlands meet the Arctic Ocean at the continent's northernmost point. More than 3,000 miles (4,800 km) to the south, the Hawai'ian islands are made up of huge underwater volcanoes sticking out of the ocean.

Bighorn sheep are found in many parts of the West. Their ability to live in harsh environments is a symbol of the West's rugged nature. There is a mountain range in Montana and Wyoming called the Bighorn Mountains.

The Pacific coast stretches from the beaches of Southern California to the coastal mountains of Washington and continues along Alaska. The coastal mountain ranges are home to evergreen and **deciduous** forests, and North America's only **temperate rainforest**. Further east, the largest mountain range in North America cuts through Idaho, Montana, Wyoming, Colorado, and Utah. The height of the Rocky Mountains creates a natural barrier for humans, animals, and even weather systems. On the east side of the Rockies, the **Great Plains** begin. In the middle, western deserts get hotter than anywhere else in the country.

Major Landmarks of the West

The many different landforms overlapping throughout the West have created some of the most iconic natural **landmarks** in the United States. The Grand Canyon is the most famous of all. More than a billion years ago, the area was a mountain range taller than the Rockies. Over time, water **eroded** these mountains away. The flat land left behind eroded even more, creating the longest and deepest canyon in North America.

Wyoming, Yellowstone National Park
Water falling through cracks in the earth at Yellowstone boils when it meets **magma**. This has created more than 300 **geysers** and 10,000 other **geothermal** features. It is also home to an active volcano. Yellowstone was the world's first national park.

🌿 The Paiute American Indians call the Grand Canyon *Kaibab*. This means "mountain lying down" or "mountain turned upside down" in their language.

Hawai'i, Mauna Kea

The dormant, or inactive, volcano rises 13,796 feet (4,205 meters) above sea level. There is another 19,700 feet (6,000 m) underwater. All together, Mauna Kea is the tallest mountain on Earth.

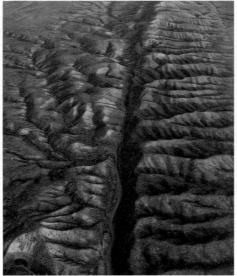

California, San Andreas Fault

The San Andreas Fault is an 800-mile (1,300-km) long crack where the Earth's crust slides in opposite directions. These plates have moved up to 2 inches (5 centimeters) per year since the early 20th century. This movement has caused powerful earthquakes in the area.

Alaska, Malaspina

Malaspina is made up of many small **glaciers**. It is 50 miles (80 km) long, 1,000 feet (300 m) thick, and it covers 1,500 square miles (3,900 square kilometers). Malaspina is so large that the entire glacier can only be seen from space.

Arizona, Grand Canyon

The bottom of the Grand Canyon is about 2 billion years old.

The Grand Canyon became a national park in 1919.

The Grand Canyon is 6,000 feet (1,800 m) deep, enough to fit the height of 4 Empire State Buildings.

Major Biomes of the West

Biomes are natural areas defined by the types of plant and animal life that call them home. Human activity can cause biomes to change, making it difficult for plants and animals to survive. The West is divided into seven major biomes. Protecting these areas is important for conserving the world's natural environments.

Mapping the Biomes of the West

Use the map below and the information on the next page to answer the following questions.

1. Which state has the most biomes?

2. What is the only state with tropical rainforest biome?

3. How many states have a desert biome?

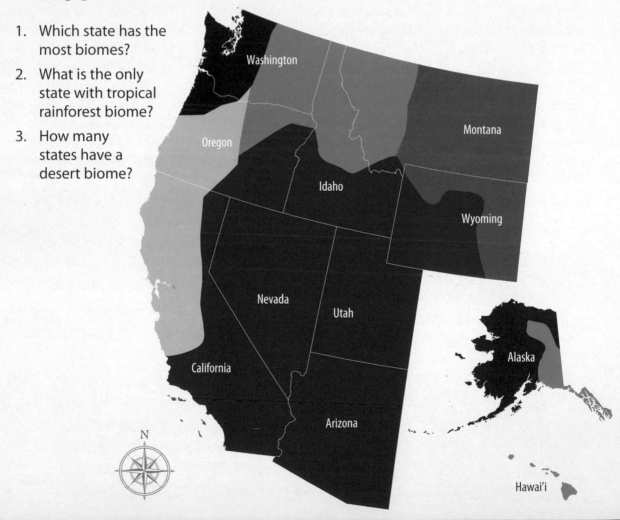

Temperate Rainforest

Climate: Cool, wet, humid

Vegetation: Redwood, shrubs, moss

Temperature: 15° to 65° Fahrenheit
(−9° to 18° Celsius)

Deciduous Forest

Climate: Seasonal

Vegetation: Dense leafy trees, flowers

Temperature: −22° to 86°F (−30° to 30°C)

Coniferous Forest

Climate: Seasonal

Vegetation: Evergreen Trees

Temperature: −40° to 68°F (−40° to 20°C)

Grasslands

Climate: Dry, seasonal

Vegetation: Grasses

Temperature: −4° to 86°F
(−20° to 30°C)

Tundra

Climate: Cold, dry

Vegetation: Shrubs, lichen

Temperature: −40° to 64°F
(−40° to 18°C)

Desert

Climate: Hot, dry

Vegetation: Water-retaining
                 plants, cacti

Temperature: 100°F
(38°C)

Tropical Rainforest

Climate: Hot, wet, humid

Vegetation: Large variety of tropical plants
                 and trees

Temperature: 68° to 77°F
(20° to 25°C)

Salmon are a key food source for grizzly bears in western forest ecosystems.

Ecosystems of the West

Within a biome, plants and animals live together, relying on each other and their surroundings for survival. This is an ecosystem. A tidal pool is an example of a small ecosystem in the West. When seawater pools on rocks along the shore, animals such as fish and **crustaceans** move in to find food and shelter. An example of a large ecosystem is a pine forest where mammals, birds, insects, fish, and plants all live together. A single tree can support a small ecosystem within the larger forest ecosystem.

Food for Thought

Ecosystems work in cycles to support all of the species living together. Food drives this cycle of life. Plants grow, relying on sunlight and nutrients in the soil. When a **herbivore** eats the plant, these nutrients are passed on to that animal. The nutrients are passed on again when a **carnivore** eats the herbivore. Eventually, the carnivore dies. Its body then **decomposes**. The soil soaks up the nutrients from the animal's body. This **fertilizes** new plant growth and starts the food cycle all over again.

Food Cycle

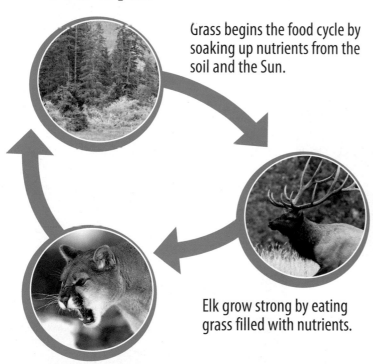

Grass begins the food cycle by soaking up nutrients from the soil and the Sun.

Elk grow strong by eating grass filled with nutrients.

Mountain lions gain nutrients from eating the elk's meat. They return the nutrients to the soil when they die.

Major Rivers of the West

Rivers act as natural boundaries. The powerful rushing water changes the landscape. People, animals, and plants travel along rivers, moving from one ecosystem to another. The West is constantly changing with the power of its rivers.

The third longest river in North America is the Mississippi River. It is fed by other large rivers, such as the Arkansas River and the Missouri River. These rivers flow from the Rocky Mountains, forming the boundary of the West.

GREENLAND

CANADA

UNITED STATES

MEXICO

Arizona, Colorado River
The Colorado flows 1,450 miles (2,300 km) from Colorado through Utah and Arizona. It carves through the rocks of the Grand Canyon along its route. So much of its water is used in the West that, in some years, it runs dry before reaching the sea.

Alaska, Yukon River
The third longest river in North America flows 1,980 miles (3,187 km) through Alaska and into the Bering Sea. Each year, millions of salmon swim up the river in the world's largest salmon **migration**.

Montana, Missouri River
The 2,250 mile (3,621 km) Missouri is North America's longest river. The Missouri drains water from one sixth of the country.

Washington, Columbia River
The 1,240-mile (2,000-km) long Columbia River drains an area almost the size of France from the Rocky Mountains to the Pacific Ocean.

California, San Joaquin River
Almost 95 percent of California's second longest river's course has been changed by human activity. Dams have caused 60 miles (97 km) to run dry, while fish and wildlife **populations** have disappeared from the area.

River Facts

65 % of drinking water in the United States comes from rivers.

3,902 miles (6,275 km) – combined length of the Missouri and Mississippi Rivers, which together make up the longest river system in the United States.

It takes **6 gallons** (23 liters) of fresh water to grow one serving of lettuce.

The **Colorado River** *travels through southwestern United States and northwestern Mexico and is home to the famous* **Hoover Dam.**

Rivers that can be traveled by canoe, kayak, or raft are owned by the American public.

Mammals of the West

The West is home to a wide variety of animal life. These animals play an important role in the ecosystems of the West. Many are symbols of the areas they call home. Some of the West's most iconic animals, such as the bighorn sheep, the cougar, and the gray wolf, are **endangered** species.

Wyoming, Bison
Millions of bison once roamed the Great Plains. By 1889, they were hunted almost to extinction. Conservation efforts in recent years have helped the bison population recover.

Alaska, Moose
The Alaskan moose is the largest animal in the deer family.

Hawai'i, Monk Seal
The Hawai'ian monk seal is an endangered species. Hawai'ians call it `Ilio holo I ka uaua, which means, "dog who runs in the water."

California, Gray Whale
Every year, thousands of Gray Whales swim past California on their journey from Alaska to Mexico.

Arizona, Ringtailed Cat
The ringtailed cat is mostly active at night, taking advantage of the cooler temperatures in the desert.

Nevada, Desert Bighorn Sheep

Desert bighorn sheep live in the mountains of Nevada's deserts. They use their thick horns to break open cacti for food.

Utah, Rocky Mountain Elk

Rocky mountain elk communicate using a variety of calls, such as bugles, barks, and squeals. Elk used to live all over North America. Today, they are only found in the West.

Washington, Orca

The orca was named Washington's official marine mammal after a campaign by second graders. Orcas live in large family groups called pods.

Idaho, Appaloosa Horse

Appaloosas are spotted horses that were important to the American Indians of Idaho. They are strong, fast horses adapted to life on the open ranges of the West.

Oregon, American Beaver

Oregon is nicknamed the Beaver State. American beavers are known as "nature's engineer" because they build dams and lodges.

Montana, Grizzly Bear

Grizzly bears are powerful **omnivores**. They can grow to 8 feet (2.4 m) tall and weigh 1,500 pounds (680 kilograms).

Reptiles and Amphibians of the West

Reptiles and amphibians are cold-blooded animals that often feed on insects, rodents, plants, and each other. Amphibians live in or near water, where they lay their eggs. In dry areas such as deserts, amphibians dig themselves into the ground to gather moisture from the soil. Reptiles lay their eggs on land. Their skin is made of scales that do not need moisture. This helps them survive in deserts and other dry areas. Reptiles and amphibians can be found in large populations, playing a central role in the food cycle.

In the Pacific, **Leatherback Turtles** have declined by **90**%

Pacific **Hawksbill Turtles** have declined **80**%

Official State Reptile/Amphibian

Arizona, Arizona Ridge-nosed Rattlesnake	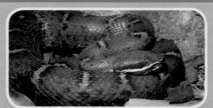	The Arizona ridge-nosed rattlesnake is a **threatened** species that **camouflages** itself in rocky or leafy areas. It uses venom to kill its prey.
California and Nevada, Desert Tortoise		The desert tortoise can live up to 100 years. It spends about 95 percent of its life in underground burrows. It is a threatened species.
Wyoming, Horned Toad		When threatened by predators, a horned toad, or horned lizard, will flatten out and blend in with the rocky ground.

Unofficial State Reptile/Amphibian

Alaska,
Leatherback Turtle

Leatherbacks are the largest turtles on Earth, weighing up to 2,000 pounds (900 kg). The endangered turtles travel thousands of miles (km) through the ocean each year.

Idaho,
Tiger Salamander

Tiger salamanders are large amphibians that grow up to 13 inches (33 cm). They spend most of their time in underground burrows near streams, ponds, or lakes.

Hawai'i,
Hawksbill Turtle

The endangered hawksbill turtle uses its long, beak-like mouth to dig food, such as sea sponges, out of coral reefs.

Montana, Pacific
Tree Frog

Pacific tree frogs are also known as Pacific chorus frogs because of the calls they make. They can be heard singing throughout much of the western United States.

Oregon,
Common Kingsnake

The common kingsnake can be found throughout much of North America. It is a **constrictor** that eats **venomous** snakes, lizards, and mice.

Utah,
Desert Iguana

The desert iguana can change its skin color to absorb the sunlight it needs to stay warm. The large tail makes up three quarters of the iguana's entire body length.

Washington,
Western Rattlesnake

Venomous western rattlesnakes are only active for about six months each year. They hibernate in underground dens throughout the winter.

Birds of the West

The West is home to a wide variety of birds that play an important role in the food cycle, even helping **pollinate** plants. Scientists often study bird populations to understand the health of entire ecosystems. Threatened or endangered birds in the West include two of the largest birds in America, the California condor and the golden eagle.

Wyoming, Western Meadowlark

The western meadowlark is well known for its flute-like song. It is also the official state bird of Kansas, Montana, Nebraska, North Dakota, and Oregon.

Idaho, Peregrine Falcon

Idaho is the only state with an official **raptor**. The peregrine falcon is the fastest animal in the world. It hunts other birds in the air at speeds faster than 200 miles (320 km) per hour.

One type of peregrine falcon only lives on the islands of Alaska.

The nene used to live on all of the Hawai'ian islands, but it can only be found on three of the islands today.

Cactus wrens are known to destroy the nests and eggs of other birds.

Utah, California Gull

California gulls saved Utah's crops from a **plague** of crickets in 1848. Today, there is a Sea Gull Monument in Salt Lake City, honoring the bird.

California, California Quail

In the summer, California quails live in pairs, but in the winter, as many as 200 group together.

Washington, American Goldfinch

The American goldfinch is also known as the willow goldfinch or the wild canary. It is also the state bird of Iowa and New Jersey.

Arizona, Cactus Wren

The cactus wren lives in desert areas, building its nest in tall cacti. The needles of the cactus help protect the wren's nest from predators.

Nevada, Mountain Bluebird

Mountain bluebirds are comfortable in colder climates, like Nevada's highlands. They can travel in flocks up to 50 birds.

Mother and father California gulls take turns taking care of their eggs. They each stay in the nest for three to four hours at a time.

California quails can survive a long time without drinking water. They can receive moisture by eating insects and plants.

The western meadowlark uses its beak to dig for insects in dirt and bark.

Alaska, Willow Ptarmigan

The willow ptarmigan lives in the short grasses and brush of the Alaskan tundra. Its camouflage coat changes from light brown in the summer to snow white in the winter.

Hawai'i, Nene

The nene is an endangered species, also know as the Hawai'ian goose. It is adapted to live on the state's volcanic slopes. It has longer toes and weaker wings than most other geese.

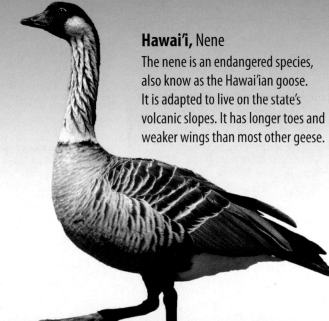

Plants of the West

From short grasses to gigantic pine trees, desert cacti, waving palm trees, and underwater kelp, all plants are important to life. Plants turn sunlight into nutrients that are then passed on through the food cycle. They also create oxygen for animals and humans to breathe. Plants are found in great numbers throughout the West. However, some important species, such as the California redwood, are endangered.

Alaska
Forget-me-nots are wildflowers that bloom during Alaska's short summers. The blue flowers grow in rocky places high in the Alaskan mountains.

Arizona
Saguaro Cactus Blossoms grow up to 40 feet (12 m) tall. It is the largest type of cacti in the United States. The white blossoms open for one day before they turn into red fruit.

65% of all plants in the West can be used as medicine.

The Oregon grape is known for its ability to survive in polluted environments.

Idaho
Syringa Mock Orange is a shrub that grows up to 10 feet (3 m) tall. It is called mock orange because the flowers smell like orange blossoms.

California
California Poppies bloom in early spring, covering California's hills in orange, peach, red, yellow, and pink. They are also called *copa de oro*, which means "cup of gold" in Spanish.

Hawai'i
Hawai'ian Yellow Hibiscus is endangered. Only about 60 plants still grow in nature.

Nevada
Sagebrush is well known for its pleasant smell. A sagebrush bush can grow up to 12 feet (3.7 m) high and produces small yellow or white flowers.

Oregon
Oregon Grape has thick, shiny leaves and dark blue berries. Its small, delicate flowers bloom in early summer.

Montana
Bitterroot is a pink wildflower. American Indians used the roots of this plant for food, mixing them with berries to make them taste sweet.

Saguaro cacti can live up to 200 years.

Indian paintbrush survives by taking nutrients from the roots of other plants.

Utah
Sego Lily is a white flower that grows in Utah's grasslands. In the 1800s, when settlers had trouble finding food, they survived by eating sego lily roots.

Wyoming
Indian Paintbrush looks like it has been dipped in red paint. These wildflowers are sometimes called painted cups or desert paintbrushes.

Washington
Coast Rhododendrons grow in round clusters of 20 or more pink, bell-shaped flowers.

Challenges Facing the West

In the forests of the West, wetlands, grasslands, deserts, and marine environments are going through major changes. As these areas change, the plants and animals that live there must change as well. Across the region, organizations are working to **conserve** threatened and endangered ecosystems and species.

In 1872, Yellowstone became the first national park in the world. Since then, it has provided a place for plants and animals to thrive in their natural environment. While national parks are protected, most natural areas in the West are not. Some threats to western forests are natural. **Invasive** species, such as bark beetle, and wildfires kill millions of trees every year.

In 1850, there were almost 2 million acres (800,000 hectares) acres of ancient coast redwood forests. Today, less than 5 percent of these forests remain.

Human Impact

Human activity is the greatest challenge to natural environments in the West. As people move to new areas, they use up more land and natural resources.

Growing cities and towns take away key **habitats** for plants and animals. Farming can also destroy habitats and introduce diseases that harm **native** species. Logging has wiped out millions of acres (hectares) of forest. **Carbon dioxide** from cars and factories has caused rising temperatures, changing weather patterns, and habitat destruction around the world.

🌿 By the late 1960s, about 90 percent of the original redwoods had been cut down by loggers.

Redwood Forest

The coast redwood tree is the tallest plant in the world. The redwood forest is home to several threatened and endangered species, such as the bald eagle, brown pelican, northern spotted owl, and chinook and coho salmon.

The coast redwood can grow to more than 350 feet (107 m) tall and can live for more than 2,000 years.

Redwoods are known to create their own rain by storing moisture in the treetops.

Large redwoods are so strong that they can live through forest fires.

Endangered Species Spotlight

The bighorn sheep is one of the most important endangered animals in the western United States. It had a North American population as high as 2 million at the beginning of the 19th century. Today, there are less than 70,000 bighorn sheep. Many of the remaining bighorn sheep are in California and Arizona. In 1996, the bighorn sheep was placed on the federal endangered species list. This has helped keep the population stable by protecting them from poachers and pollution.

In 1987, there were only 22 California condors left in nature. Hunting and habitat destruction had pushed North America's largest bird to near extinction. All of the remaining condors were placed in captivity in an effort to save the species. Five years later, the birds were **reintroduced** to their natural habitat. Today, there are more than 200 wild California condors in the West.

One of the main threats to bighorn sheep is disease spread from nearby sheep farms.

The gray wolf is the largest **canine** in the world. In the past, there were up to 2 million gray wolves worldwide. They were hunted to near extinction. Today, there are only about 200,000 gray wolves left in nature.

In 1995, a group of scientists captured 66 wolves in Canada and released them in Yellowstone and Idaho. There had been no wolves in Yellowstone since the 1970s. Today, the wolf population is thriving, with about 100 wolves in Yellowstone National Park.

Cougars once lived across North America. Today, aside from a small population in Florida, cougars are only found in the West.

Get Involved

One way to support the growth of animal populations is to join conservation groups that preserve animal habitats. Threatened raptor species, such as the bald eagle and the California condor, can be injured or killed by human activity. One major threat to raptors in the West is poisoning. Chemicals such as lead can pollute rivers and lakes, as well as the animals that live in them. When birds such as condors or eagles eat these animals, they can die from the poison in the meat. There are many organizations that help injured animals recover.

You can help these birds by adopting your own California condor. The Ventana Wildlife Society monitors the population, rescues poisoned birds, and supplies food to condors living in nature. By adopting a condor, you can help a threatened bird grow, and watch it flourish in its natural habitat.

For more information, visit the Ventana Wildlife Society at www.mycondor.org, and talk to your parents, teacher, and classmates about adopting a California condor.

Activity

The American beaver can change the landscape enough to create new ecosystems. A beaver cuts down trees, to turn a flowing river into a still pond. Fish that have been trapped by the dam now live in a pond instead of a river. Insects breed around ponds. This provides food for fish and other animals, such as reptiles and amphibians. Birds and mammals then move in to feed on the abundant life in and around the beaver pond. When completing this activity, think about how one species can affect so many others in an ecosystem.

A beaver's teeth never stop growing. Chewing wood keeps them trimmed down to a manageable size.

Make an Ecosystem Web

Use this book, and research on the Internet, to create an ecosystem web.

1. Find an endangered plant or animal that lives in the West. Refer to previous pages in this book for examples. Think about its habitat.

2. Find at least three living things that are found in the same habitat. This could include plants, insects, amphibians, reptiles, birds, or mammals.

3. How do each of these living things interact with each other? Do they provide food or shelter for the other plants or animals?

4. Begin linking these living things together to show which plants and animals rely on each other for food or shelter. Use red arrows for food and blue arrows for shelter. The arrows should point toward the plant or animal receiving the food or shelter.

5. Once your ecosystem web is complete, think about how removing the endangered plant or animal would affect the other living things in the web. What would be some of the results?

Sample Ecosystem Web

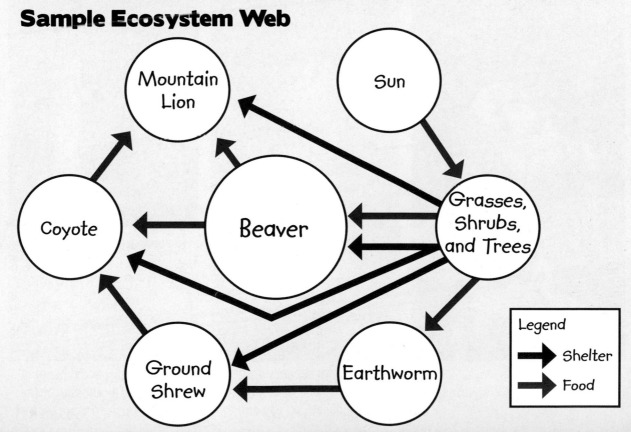

Quiz

1 What two oceans border the West?

2 What Hawai'ian mountain is the tallest on Earth?

3 What is the world's largest turtle?

4 What is the longest river in the United States?

5 What is the largest type of deer?

6 How many major biomes are found in the West?

7 Which state has an official raptor?

8 What was the world's first National Park?

9 What type of tree can create its own rain?

10 How many California condors were left in nature in 1987?

ANSWERS: 1. Pacific and Arctic 2. Mauna Kea 3. The leatherback turtle 4. The Missouri River 5. The Alaskan moose 6. Seven 7. Idaho (peregrine falcon) 8. Yellowstone National Park 9. The coast redwood 10. 22

Key Words

camouflages: to blend in with the surroundings

canine: member of the dog family

carbon dioxide: a gas that can be toxic in large amounts, and causes climate change

carnivore: an animal that mainly eats meat

conserve: protect from harm

constrictor: a snake that kills its prey through suffocation

crustaceans: shelled sea creatures like crabs and lobsters

deciduous: trees that lose leaves in winter

decomposes: when something rots and its nutrients go back to the soil

endangered: in danger of disappearing

eroded: washed away by wind or water

fertilizes: gives nutrients to the soil

geothermal: made with heat from the earth

geysers: hot springs that send water shooting into the air when it boils

glaciers: giant slabs of ice that move and grow slowly over millions of years

Great Plains: a wide open area of flat grassland east of the Rock Mountains

habitats: places where something lives

herbivore: an animal that mainly eats plants

invasive: a species that moves into new areas and destroys populations of other species

landforms: a feature on Earth's surface, like a mountain, a hill, or a valley

landmarks: a famous landform or object

magma: hot liquid rock from Earth's core

migration: a number of animals moving together

native: originating in a certain place

omnivores: animals that eat both plants and meat

plague: a large number of insects causing destruction

pollinate: the way plants use pollen to reproduce

populations: a group of the same species in one area

raptor: a bird that hunts other animals

reintroduced: brought a species back to an area

temperate rainforest: a forest that gets a great deal of rain but is not tropical

threatened: a species that could become endangered

venomous: an animal that uses poison to kill its prey

Index

Log on to www.av2books.com

AV² by Weigl brings you media enhanced books that support active learning. Go to www.av2books.com, and enter the special code found on page 2 of this book. You will gain access to enriched and enhanced content that supplements and complements this book. Content includes video, audio, weblinks, quizzes, a slide show, and activities.

AV² Online Navigation

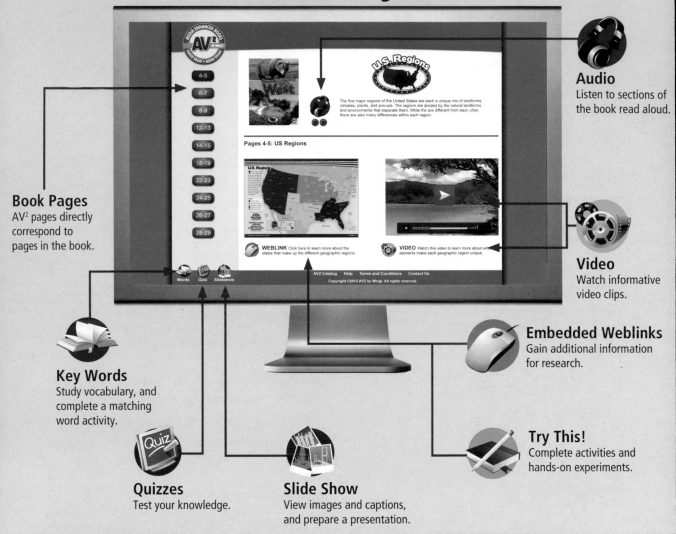

Book Pages
AV² pages directly correspond to pages in the book.

Audio
Listen to sections of the book read aloud.

Video
Watch informative video clips.

Embedded Weblinks
Gain additional information for research.

Key Words
Study vocabulary, and complete a matching word activity.

Try This!
Complete activities and hands-on experiments.

Quizzes
Test your knowledge.

Slide Show
View images and captions, and prepare a presentation.

AV² was built to bridge the gap between print and digital. We encourage you to tell us what you like and what you want to see in the future.

Sign up to be an AV² Ambassador at www.av2books.com/ambassador.

Due to the dynamic nature of the Internet, some of the URLs and activities provided as part of AV² by Weigl may have changed or ceased to exist. AV² by Weigl accepts no responsibility for any such changes. All media enhanced books are regularly monitored to update addresses and sites in a timely manner. Contact AV² by Weigl at 1-866-649-3445 or av2books@weigl.com with any questions, comments, or feedback.